Reading and Writing is Childsplay

Jan Morrow

Longman

*This material is also part of
Head Start to Learning.*

LONGMAN GROUP UK LIMITED
*Longman House
Burnt Mill, Harlow, Essex CM20 2JE, England
and Associated Companies throughout the World.*

First published 1989
ISBN 0 582 05378 1

Set in Linotype 11/12pt Frutiger 45 Light

*Printed and bound in Great Britain by
Courier International Ltd, Tiptree, Essex*

General contents

General introduction

Parents as teachers

The first years of life are a very special time — for a child and for his or her parents. More than at any other time, it is the parents who are responsible for shaping the child's world. Television, playgroup, radio, colourful books and marvellous toys bombard the young child with experiences and stimulate his or her natural curiosity. It is this curiosity that is the key to the child's approach to the world. How many times a day do we answer questions about 'Why?', 'What?' or 'Where?' As parents, we already offer a wealth of information and experiences, so why not the basics of reading, and writing as well?

There is a great deal of positive and constructive help that parents can offer young children, based on common sense and the ideas and guidelines set out in this book. Many young children develop reading and writing skills successfully at home. There is no reason at all why children need to be 5+ in order to start; the intellectual leap needed is a matter of development, not age. This development can be encouraged by the games and activities described here.

One of the greatest advantages that parents can offer young children at home is time. At home, the child can be the single focus of the parent's attention. Learning that is rooted in the caring, loving framework of home can blossom. But loving care is essential. Impatience and pressure from the parent will kill the interest, enthusiasm and curiosity which are at the heart of all successful learning.

What is in this book?

This book contains a wide range of games and play activities designed to be fun for young children. As a by-product of playing the games, the child will be picking up skills and concepts that will help the development of reading and writing. But it is the fun that counts! If the child seems at all bored by a particular game or activity, stop at once.

There are two sections in the book, one dealing with reading and one with writing. Each section has an introduction giving more details about the use of the activities described. But a quick glance will show that there is a lot of material. Most children will only ever use a part of it. Don't feel that you have wasted your time if you haven't covered every activity in a given section.

Each section is divided into developmental stages. Don't push your child into going further than he or she is ready to. Stop at the first signs of 'struggle'. Leave it for a few months and try again.

Most of the activities have a 'make the game' part. On the whole, this is the parent's responsibility, but don't forget that children love to get involved in helping. As you will see, the equipment required for the games is very basic. Nearly everything can easily be found around the house, and no great artistic talent or construction skills are needed.

Reading

Contents

Introduction

How to use the reading games listed in this book

Stage one:
Pre-reading games and activities 10

Stage two:
Introducing content words 20

Stage three:
Introducing connecting words and simple sentences 34

* These are phonic activities

Stage four:
The beginnings of a phonic approach to reading 47

Introduction

As parents we are aware that learning to read is very important for our children. We also realise that many children show an interest in and a love of books at an early age, and that many seem ready to read long before they are ready for school. This section of the book contains over eighty games and activities which are designed to help your child to learn to read in an informal and fun way. In addition, there is advice and information on how to approach the introduction of reading.

But before starting the games and activities, how many of the following questions can you answer yes to?

Do you make time to talk to your child?
Do you listen to your child?
Do you read to your child?
Does your child see you reading?
Does your child have his own book shelf, where colourful, well-illustrated books are available?
Do you take your child to the local library and encourage him to choose books?
Have you discovered if there are any story telling sessions at the local library?
Do you sing to your child?
Do you tell lots of nursery rhymes?
Do you use children's television programmes to stimulate conversation?
Do you provide opportunity for creative play?
Does your child communicate and play with other adults and children, perhaps at playgroup?

The more of these your child is involved in, the more useful the games and activities in this book will be.

How to use the reading games listed in this book

These games and activities should be enjoyed. Don't force your child to participate. If he prefers to play all day on his bike in the garden, so be it. Wait until the next wet day and see if he seems interested then. Keep it fun and keep the time allotted to each activity short, so that the child doesn't become bored.

The activities and games are divided into four stages and each stage should be developed before moving on to the next. Here are a few points to remember:

Don't rush through the list of games.
Keep a flexible approach and spend as much time as is necessary on each set of activities.
Move slowly and don't expect to cover all the games in each stage.
Only when you feel your child is totally confident and copes easily with the activities and games at one stage should you move on to the next.

Stage one:
Pre-reading games and activities

Stage one consists of pre-reading games and activities designed to provide a strong foundation of concepts and skills which it is necessary to develop before any 'reading' can take place.

If your child doesn't go further than this stage, don't worry. He will still have acquired a depth of knowledge which will help him tremendously when he starts to read. The games at this stage are designed to help with such things as visual discrimination and comparison, training the eye to move from left to right, the development of language, the improvement of memory, and the encouragement of auditory skills through listening to everyday sounds.

Stage two:
Introducing content words

Stage three:
Introducing connecting words and simple sentences

Stages two and three contain activities and games arranged around the look-and-say approach to teaching reading. There are many different methods of teaching a child to read but basically they can be divided into three types:

> Look-and-say whole word
> Look-and-say whole sentence
> Phonic – based on individual sounds

Variations and combinations of these three approaches are used in most schools and there are arguments for and against each of them. However, many schools start with a look-and-say approach, with phonics being introduced when the child has established a basic reading vocabulary. Stages two, three and four therefore follow this sequence.

Look-and-say

Look-and-say simply means that the child memorises and reads a whole word without first breaking the word down into letters. The child learns to read and see 'cat' not 'cuh-a-tuh'. This allows the child to start reading simple books quickly and easily, thus building up confidence and enthusiasm for reading. Stage two uses this approach to introduce individual 'content' words, such as 'mummy' or 'house', while stage

three starts to put the content words together with simple 'connecting' words such as 'and'.

Phonics

Phonics are the sounds which make up a word. For example 'duh-a-guh' (dog) contains three sounds. Phonics should be introduced very gradually. Most children find it very difficult to hear the individual sounds within a word since they are only used to hearing whole words, sentences and phrases. Some phonic games are included in stages one to three. (They are marked with an asterisk * in the contents list and on the page where they are described.)

The phonic games in stage two are an extension of the auditory games found in stage one. They encourage the child to 'listen' to the initial sounds of words, and help him to distinguish and discriminate between sounds. At this stage, the games avoid relating sounds to letters of the alphabet. This is not to say that a child will not notice individual letters while he is 'reading'. Obviously he will be curious and his curiosity must be satisfied. So if he asks, simply give him the sound but not the name of the letter e.g. a, buh, cuh. Never, 'ay', 'bee', 'see'. A full list of letter sounds can be found in stage four.

Stage three phonic games do start to relate sounds to individual letters. They aim to help the child to recognise letters of the alphabet and some of the sounds with which they are associated.

Stage four:
The beginnings of a phonic approach to reading

Stage four contains games and activities which extend the range of the phonics introduced at previous stages and lead the child to begin to break down simple words into sounds.

Stage one:
Pre-reading activities

Silhouette matching

Collect together:

- a sheet of paper 35cm by 30cm.
- a sheet of thick paper or card 35cm by 30cm.
- a pencil.
- a thick black felt tip pen.
- glue and a glue brush.
- scissors.
- a children's picture colouring book or old magazines.

Make the game

1 Look through the picture book or old magazines and find about six or seven simple pictures of familiar objects, e.g. a dog, a chair, a flower.
2 Very carefully cut round the objects you have chosen and glue them on to the sheet of card. Alternatively if you are good at drawing, draw some objects straight on to the card.

3 When the glue has dried, carefully cut round the objects and, using them as templates, draw round each one on to the sheet of paper.
4 Turn the outline drawings on the paper into black silhouettes by colouring them in with the felt tip pen.

Play the game

Ask the child to match and cover up the black silhouettes with the correct objects.

Milk-top threading

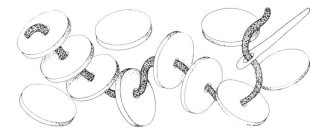

Collect together:

- lots of clean milk bottle tops.
- a ball of wool.
- a darning needle – the type which is large and blunt ended.
- scissors.

Play the game

Thread the needle with wool. Tie a knot at the end and thread the milk tops on to the wool. Even very young children find it easy to 'sew' milk bottle tops and the finished product could be turned into a necklace.

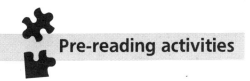

Spot the difference

Collect together:

- a piece of card 6cm by 6cm.
- a piece of paper 30cm by 15cm.
- scissors.
- a felt tip pen.
- a pencil.

Make the game

1 Take the piece of card and make a template of an animal or everyday object, e.g. a fish. If you are not very artistic, cut out a picture from a magazine, mount it on card and cut round it to make the template.
2 Use the template to draw the outline shape of the fish (or whatever you have chosen) several times on to the piece of paper.
3 As accurately as you can, draw identical details on to each fish, e.g. a fin, an eye, a tail pattern etc. Create a difference by missing out some of the detail on one of the fishes. The younger the child the more obvious the missing detail needs to be.

Play the game

Give the child a pencil and ask him to find the fish with something missing. He could then draw in the missing detail or simply draw a ring around the appropriate fish.

Making jigsaws

Collect together:

- old magazines, comics, or birthday/Christmas cards.
- scissors.
- a piece of card the same size as the picture you choose.
- glue and a glue brush.
- a pencil.
- a large envelope.

Make the game

1 Find a colourful picture and cut it out.
2 Stick the picture on to the card and when it is

dry cut it into pieces. Obviously the younger the child the fewer the pieces.

Play the game

Ask your child to put the picture back together again. When she has finished she can pop the jigsaw into the envelope to keep it safe until next time.

Colander threading

Collect together:

- a kitchen colander.
- a pair of boot laces.

Play the game

Give the child a long boot lace with a knot at one end. Ask her to thread the boot lace through the holes in the kitchen colander. If you can't obtain boot laces, use shoe laces instead.

✗ The shopping memory game

This game is an old favourite and can be played by 2 or more players. You start the game by saying,

  'I went shopping one morning and I bought a cabbage.'

The next player then repeats the phrase and adds something to the shopping list, e.g.

  'I went shopping one morning and I bought a cabbage and a bottle of milk.'

The game continues with each player in turn adding another item to the shopping list. This is quite a difficult game, so be prepared to help little ones and don't expect them to get the shopping list in the right order.

Matching pairs game

Collect together:

- 12 small pieces of card, 8cm by 8cm.
- 6 pairs of identical pictures taken from comics or magazines.
- glue and glue brush.
- scissors.

Make the game

1 Trim all the pictures so that they are just slightly smaller than the pieces of card.
2 Glue each picture on to a card.

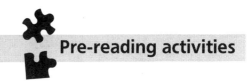

Play the game

Spread the cards on a table, picture-side down. Each player takes a turn at lifting two of the cards. If the pictures are the same he can keep the cards; if they aren't, he returns them face down on the table. The winner is the one who collects the most pairs. This is a good memory game as the child needs to remember where certain cards are in order to make up a pair.

Picture lotto

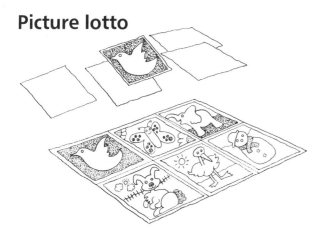

Collect together:

- 4 sheets of card 24cm by 20cm.
- a ruler.
- a pencil.
- scissors.
- 2 identical children's comics.
- glue and a glue brush.

Make the game (for two players)

1 Using the pencil and ruler divide each piece of card into 6 identical sections. Each section should be 8cm by 10cm.
2 Look through one of the children's comics and find 12 colourful pictures of comic characters. Find the same pictures in the second comic and cut out all 24 pictures. The pictures need to be small enough to fit easily into the 8cm by 10cm spaces on the cards.
3 Take the pictures from the first comic and glue them on to the marked section on 2 of the cards.Put the cards on one side to dry.
4 Take the identical pictures from the second comic and stick them on to the sections on the remaining 2 cards. When the glue has dried cut out each section of these two cards so that you have 12 separately mounted pictures.

Play the game

Each of the two players has a complete card with six comic characters stuck on it.

Spread the loose pictures on a table top, picture-side down. Each player takes it in turn to pick a picture and try to match it with those on her card. If it is identical she places it on top of the picture on her card;if not, she returns it face down on the table. The winner is the first to cover her pictures.

What's missing?

Collect together:

- a large tray.
- a tea towel
- a collection of small objects e.g. a toothbrush, a cup, an apple, a toy car, etc.

Play the game

Put four objects on to the tray. Ask the child to look at them. Cover the objects up with the tea towel and while the child closes his eyes, remove one of the objects and put it behind your back.

Remove the tea towel, ask the child to open his eyes and tell you what's missing. When he guesses correctly, return the missing item and make the game a little harder by adding a 5th object to the tray. You can of course add as many or as few objects to the tray as you feel necessary.

Children also love to remove the items themselves while mummy closes her eyes and then tries to guess correctly.

Simple riddles

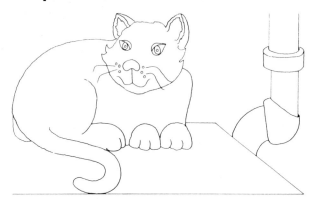

Play the game

Ask the child to answer some very simple riddles for you. Make sure the subject matter of the riddle is very familiar to the child, e.g.

> Grown-up: 'What's grey and warm and furry and sleeps on top of the boiler in the kitchen?'
> Child: 'Jessicat!'

In this example the grown up is providing and using descriptive words about a familiar object, i.e. the family cat. At the same time the child is learning to listen carefully, and is extending in a receptive way her own vocabulary. When you feel the child has grasped the idea of the game, ask her to make up a riddle. At first she will find it hard not to actually name what she is thinking of, but gradually she will begin to make up descriptions for herself.

Picture story strips

Collect together:

- a strip of card, 8cm by 30cm. This will make one story strip.
- a felt tip pen.
- a ruler.

Make the game

1 Think of a very simple story. It doesn't have to be an elaborate tale, just a familiar sequence of events. Children love stories about themselves, so it could be something that has actually happened to your child.
2 In your mind divide the story up into not more than five sections, e.g.

> A girl has a packet of flower seeds.
> She puts a seed in a flower pot.
> She waters the seed and the sun shines.
> A flower grows from the pot.

3 Using a ruler and the felt tip pen divide the strip of card into equal sections. Draw the story in pictures from left to right on to the card. It doesn't matter if you aren't particularly good at drawing. Matchstick figures would do nicely.

Play the game

Ask the child to look at the story strip with you. Point to the first picture with your finger and, as you tell the story, run your finger along the bottom of the strip.

Now ask the child to tell you the story and as she does so, guide her finger from left to right along the bottom of the card.

You can build up quite a collection of story strips. Keep them together in an empty shoe box and the child will be able to look at the stories over and over again. Children may even like to make up their own stories and draw them on to strips.

You can also cut out the sections of story, jumble them up and ask the child to put them back together again in the right order.

Spin a nursery rhyme

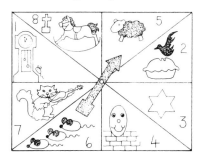

Collect together:

- 3 pieces of card, 20cm by 20cm, 40cm by 8cm and 12cm by 2cm.
- a brass paper fastener.
- a ruler.
- a felt tip pen.
- crayons.
- scissors.
- a button for each player.

Make the game

1 Draw lines to form a 'Union Jack' on the 20cm by 20cm piece of card. On the outside edge of each section of the flag draw a nursery rhyme character, e.g. Humpty Dumpty, Baa Baa Black Sheep, a Twinkle Twinkle Little Star, Three Blind Mice and so on. At the side of each character print a number. Ask your child to help you colour the pictures.
2 Make a spinner by cutting out an arrow from the 12cm by 2cm piece of card and attach it to the middle of the flag with the brass paper fastener. Make sure that it is loose enough to spin easily.
3 Using the ruler and pen divide the 40cm by 8cm strip of card into 20 sections.

Play the game

Each player takes a button and places it at the start of the 40cm strip.

The players take turns to spin the arrow. When the arrow stops spinning and points to a nursery rhyme character and number, the player must say that particular rhyme before she can move her button the appropriate number of spaces.

The buttons should be moved from left to right along the strip. The winner is the one to reach the end of the strip first.

✕ Printing

Collect together:

- empty cotton reels, potatoes cut in half, carrot tops, corks, toy bricks, etc.
- sheets of paper. (Old newspaper would do.)
- ready mixed liquid paint. 2 colours are usually sufficient.
- a paint brush or 2 old sponges and 2 plates.

To make a print

Provide the child with the objects, paper and paint.

If using paint and a paint brush the child simply covers one side of an object with paint and presses the painted surface on to the paper.

If using the sponges and plates, you put each sponge on to a plate and thoroughly soak the sponge with paint. The child presses the objects on the sponge before printing on to paper.

This activity is great fun and the child should be left to enjoy herself, but if she is printing a pattern across the paper do remind her to print from left to right.

✕ Hand puppets

Collect together:

- a sheet of card 30cm by 20cm.
- scissors.
- felt tip pens or crayons.
- 2 long cardboard tubes. The type used to hold tinfoil would be fine.
- Sellotape.

Make the game

1 Ask the child to lay one of his hands with fingers outstretched on to the sheet of card. Help him to draw round his hand with the felt tip pen in order to obtain a hand outline. Do this with both hands.

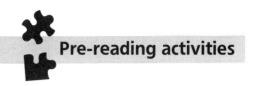

2 Cut the hand outlines out and draw faces on the palms. Stick the hand people on to the top of the cardboard tubes with some Sellotape.

Play the game

Encourage your child to make up stories and little plays for the hand people. Why not provide a puppet theatre by hanging a sheet between two kitchen chairs.

✗ The washing day game

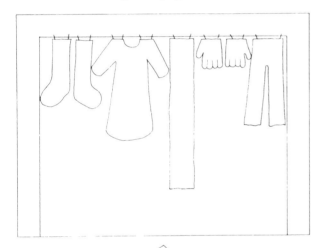

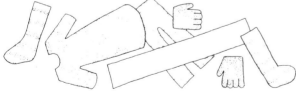

Collect together:

- a sheet of plain paper, 20cm by 30cm.
- a felt tip pen.
- some patterned paper.
- scissors.

Make the game

1 Draw a simple washing line on to the sheet of plain paper.
2 Draw and cut out several small items of clothing from the patterned paper, e.g. a dress, a pair of trousers, a scarf, a pair of gloves.
3 Using the cut-outs as templates, draw the outline of the clothes on to the washing line.

Play the game

Give the child the cut-out clothes and ask him to hang the washing out to dry by matching the cut-outs with the drawings on the line. Encourage the child to fill the washing line from left to right.

In the bag

Collect together:

- a pillow case.
- a collection of objects such as an apple, a comb, a rubber glove, etc. (Make sure that the child does not see the objects.)

Play the game

Put the objects into the pillow case. Ask the child to dip his hand into the bag and feel round for one of the objects.

Without removing the object ask him to tell you what he can feel. If he finds this difficult ask him a few questions about it, e.g. Is it soft or hard, smooth or rough?

When he has finished describing the object and has guessed what it is, he removes it from the bag and starts again.

Alternatively, the adult could put a hand in the bag and describe one of the objects to the child. Again the child should try to guess what the object is.

* Sounds lotto 1

(To make a game for two players)

Collect together:

- a cassette recorder and blank tape.
- 2 sheets of card or paper 20cm by 15cm.
- a ruler.
- a felt tip pen.
- 8 buttons.

Make the game

1 Take the cassette recorder and tape 8 familiar sounds with a short silence between each one. The sounds could include, e.g. a tap running, the telephone ringing, the door bell ringing, the dog barking, the clock ticking, the toilet flushing, hoovering, and whisking an egg.
2 Take the sheets of card and divide each one into 4 equal sections. Draw a simple picture of one of the objects which make the sounds in each section. Make sure that you do not draw the pictures in the same order as the sounds on the tape.

Play the game

Each child takes a card and a pile of buttons and listens carefully to the tape. Each time he hears a sound, he looks at his card and if he can see a picture of the object which makes the sound he places a button on top of the appropriate picture.

The winner is the one whose card is full of buttons first. Obviously one of the cards is always going to be the 'winner's' card. So before the children notice this fact, make sure that they all get a turn with that particular card. When they finally realise the game is 'fixed', start again by making a new collection of pictures and/or recordings.

*Home-made musical instruments

Home-made musical instruments are inexpensive, easy to make and great fun to play. Use them to accompany favourite nursery rhymes and songs.

Maracas

Simply fill an empty washing up liquid bottle with dried peas.

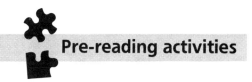

A drum

Use a saucepan and a wooden spoon.

Musical bottles

Fill 5 empty glass milk bottles with different levels of water and tap with a teaspoon. (Of course young children should always be supervised when playing with glass bottles.)

A guitar

Wrap thick rubber bands around an empty shoe box or ice cream tub.(Remove the lid first.) Create the noise by plucking the rubber bands.

A tambourine

Thread milk bottle tops on to 2 or 3 lengths of wool. Cut a large hole in the centre of a round plastic margarine lid and tie the lengths of wool to the lid.

*Stop and go!

Collect together:

- 4 or 5 items which make a noise, e.g. a whistle, a rattle, a pan and spoon.

Play the game

To start the game use two sounds only, e.g. a whistle and a rattle. Explain to the child that when the rattle shakes, she should walk around the room and when the whistle blows she should stop and stand still.

Use the rattle and the whistle alternately for a few minutes until the child is familiar with the routine. Now introduce a third sound and a third action, e.g. a clap means hop. After a while a fourth sound can be added, e.g. a bang on the pan means jump.

Be prepared to change places with your child and let her make the noises. Incidentally this is a good game for a party.

*Beat out rhythms

This is a clapping game. Start by clapping out the number of syllables in your child's name, e.g.

Kate = 1 clap.
Sophie = 2 claps.
Nicholas = 3 claps.

Sing the names as you clap and ask the child to join in.

Now try mummy and daddy, which have 2 claps each.

This activity is far harder than you may think. Little ones often don't clap rhythmically and find it hard to sing and clap at the same time. However practice makes perfect and eventually all sorts of silly clapping songs can be made up, e.g.

'The drinks song'

(Sing to the tune of Frere Jaques)

Coffee (2) Coffee (2)
Coffee (2) Coffee (2)
Lemonade (3) Lemonade (3)
CoCo (2) CoCo (2) Cola (2)
CoCo (2) CoCo (2) Cola (2)
Coffee (2) Tea (1)
Coffee (2) Tea (1)

Stage two:

Introducing content words

A 'reading readiness' check list

Here is a quick check list. If you can answer 'yes' to the following questions, then your child, regardless of age, is probably ready to start the gradual process of learning to read using the games and activities in this section.

Is your child fit and healthy, with no hearing or sight problems?

Is she a reasonably confident child with no great emotional worries at the moment?

Can she speak clearly and in sentences?

Can she remember and repeat nursery rhymes and very simple stories?

Can she hold a conversation with other adults and children?

Can she carry out simple instructions such as, 'Please go upstairs and get some clean socks from the sock drawer'?

Can she put together simple jigsaws and other manipulative toys?

Can she cope easily with the type of games and activities described in stage one?

Is she curious about things? Does she ask questions?

Does she enjoy looking at books with you and having stories read to her?

How to prepare and use 'look-and-say' cards

Cut some white cardboard into strips, 11 cm by 22 cm. You will also need a fairly thick, black, felt tip pen.

Probably the best word to start with is your child's own name. Write his or her name with the black pen on to one of the strips of card.

Apart from the initial letter of people's names, always use lower-case letters (not capitals) but do make sure that the letters are large and clear. It sometimes makes it easier for your child to memorise the words if you make each card larger and put a picture above the word. However, the picture will need to be removed after a few days, as it is important that the child learns to recognise the shape of the word without the aid of a picture.

Show the card to the child. Slowly tell her what it says and as you do so run your finger underneath the word from left to right. Never let your finger go from right to left. If you want to read the word twice, take your finger away from the card when you reach the end of the word and put it back at the beginning.

Your child will probably want to repeat the word without any prompting. But if not, ask her to say what is on the card and help her to run her finger under the word from left to right as she does so.

Repeat the whole process of reading the card to the child and asking her to read it to you.

You should aim to read the card together several times a day during the next day or two. BUT make sure that the reading sessions are very, very short. Young children are able to concentrate for only a very limited time. Be sure that you don't interrupt the child to read to you when she is playing a favourite game or happily watching television.

After a couple of days, introduce the next look-and-say card. The word should be 'mummy' or 'daddy'. The aim is to introduce and slowly build up a collection of 'family' look-and-say words. These could include the names of sisters, brothers, family pets, best friends and so on.

As well as reading the look-and-say cards, the child should be using these words in the games and activities listed in this section. For example, as well as reading the word 'daddy' from the look-and-say card the child should be:

Making the word 'daddy' out of plasticine;
Tracing the word 'daddy';
Making a 'daddy' badge;
Using the word 'daddy' in games such as lotto.

After 'family' words what then? Here are some suggestions....

Home words; table, door, bed...
Favourite toy words; Lego, bike, doll....
Animal words; dog, cat, horse...
Food words; sweets, chips, apple...
Colour words; red, blue, green...
Action words; jump, run, hop...
Place words; park, shop, playgroup, garden...

All of these are examples of 'content' words. As you can see, at this stage small connecting words such as 'is' and 'the' are not introduced. You may feel that because 'is' and 'the' are small in size that they must be easy to memorise, but this is not so. They are not easy words for a child to understand. You can't actually see an 'is' but you can see and understand a content word such as 'television'. And understanding is the key to learning. The introduction of connecting words should be left until later and is covered in stage three.

Keeping a reading record

Probably the easiest method of recording your child's reading progress at this stage is to keep the look-and-say cards together in an envelope or empty shoe box. However, as children love to look at and play with their 'words' it seems inevitable that some may get lost or badly stained and need replacing. Therefore, keep a note book as well which contains a list of the words your child knows. It is important that the cards remain clean and undamaged otherwise the child may associate a particular word with a mark on the card. For example, if the card with 'dog' on it is slightly torn in one corner, this may act as a visual clue to the word. The child wouldn't need to see the word dog he would merely respond to the tear.

Magic words

Collect together:

● 2 or 3 sheets of white paper, 21cm by 26cm.
● a white candle.
● a jar of very thin black paint.
● a paint brush.

Make the game

1 Choose a word that your child is learning at the moment, e.g. dog.
2 Use the candle to draw a dog on each of the sheets of paper. Underneath each picture, use the candle again to write the word dog. You

will need to press down quite firmly with the candle.

Play the game

Ask the child to discover the magic words and pictures by painting gently over the wax treated paper with the thin black paint. Small children are always amazed to see the magic words appearing.

Family badges

Collect together:

- cardboard discs (one for each member of the family). The discs can be made by drawing round a small coffee cup on a sheet of cardboard.
- safety pins.
- Sellotape.
- a black felt tip pen.
- crayons.
- scissors.

Make the game

Make a badge by attaching a safety pin to the back of the cardboard disc with a piece of Sellotape. Write the name of each member of your family on a badge. (Apart from the initial letter of each person's name, use lower-case letters.) Children also love to decorate the badges with patterns or pictures but do make sure that they don't obscure the words.

Play the game

Put the badges on and try to remember to wear them for at least two or three days. Grown-ups should point to the badges occasionally and ask the child to tell them what the word says.

✗ Plasticine names

Collect together:

- a sheet of card, 30cm by 20cm.
- Plasticine.
- a pencil.

Make the game

Use one of the content words you are intoducing to your child and write it in large (lower case) letters on to the piece of card.

Play the game

Help your child to make several long Plasticine snakes. Help the child use the snakes to make the word on the card by laying the Plasticine on top of the print. If the snake is a little too long or short for a particular letter you can easily add to or take away some of the Plasticine.

Do remember to encourage the child to start with the first letter of the word and help him to form the letters correctly, e.g. If one of the letters is an S the child should start by placing the Plasticine at the top of the letter.

At a later stage your child may be able to make certain words such as his own name without the aid of the printed word underneath.

Place cards

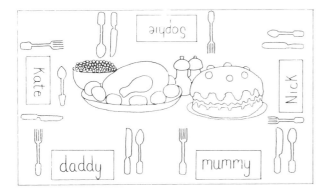

Collect together:

- strips of card, 5cm by 20cm. (You will need one strip for each member of the family.)
- a thick felt tip pen.

Make the game

Write the name of each member of your family on a strip of card. (Apart from the initial letter of each name, use lower case letters not capitals.)

Play the game

At meal times when the table is being set ask your child to use the name cards to show where each member of the family is to sit. The cards can either be put on the chairs or placed in between the knives and forks.

Labelling

Collect together:

- strips of white card, 20cm by 6cm.
- a thick black felt tip pen.
- Sellotape.

Play the game

Putting labels on to selected items found around the home is a good way of ensuring that the child sees the connection between the written word and the object it represents.

For example:
When introducing 'home words', you could write the words, television, table, chair, door etc. on to pieces of card and then sellotape them on to the objects concerned.

When using 'colour words' (introduce one colour at a time) you could give the child a handful of 'red' cards and then ask him to go round the house and put red labels on anything red he can find.

You could also label his favourite toys and put his name on his bedroom door.

A general interest table where all the items are labelled is also a good idea. The table could contain natural objects such as stones, twigs, moss and flowers. Or it could have a theme such as 'farm animals' or 'things which shine'.

The child's own creative work, paintings and models etc. can also be attractively displayed and labelled.

Tracing

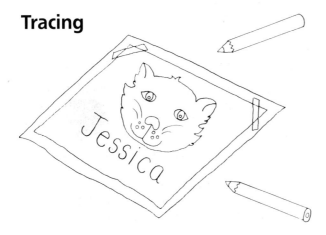

Collect together:

- sheets of white paper. (A good size would be 20cm by 18cm.)
- greaseproof paper, cut slightly smaller than the white paper.
- a black felt tip pen.
- a pencil.
- Sellotape.
- scissors.
- crayons.

Make the game

Initially the child should be given simple pictures to trace. When he has learnt how to hold the pencil correctly and has some degree of pencil control (see stage one of the writing section for information on pencil practice), you can provide him with tracing cards which contain some of the content words you are introducing.

1 Using large lower-case letters write some content words on the white paper with the felt tip pen (one word per sheet of paper). Appropriate pictures could also be drawn on to the paper but make sure that they do not obscure the letters.
2 Sellotape a sheet of the greaseproof paper on top of each word.

Play the game

Spend a little time looking at the tracing words with your child. Two or three tracing cards at any one time is probably sufficient. Give the child the pencil and ask him to trace the words for you. Ask him to name each word before and after he has traced it and do remember to help him to form his letters correctly. (See the letter chart in stage two of the writing section for details of letter formation.) During the early stages of writing it is advisable to sit with your child in order to encourage correctly formed letters.

If you have drawn some pictures the child can now colour them in.

Word lotto

(To make a game for two players)

Collect together:

- 2 pieces of white card, 24cm by 12cm.
- 12 small pieces of card, 8cm by 6cm.
- a felt tip pen.
- a ruler.

Make the the game

1 Use the ruler and the pen to divide the two large cards into 6 equal sections. Each section should be 8cm by 6 cm.
2 In each section write out one of the content words you are introducing at the moment. You will need 12 words altogether and these should be a mixture of words which the child already knows and some words which are new to him. If you feel picture clues may help your child to recognise the words, these should also be drawn on to the sections of card.
3 Write the words out for a second time on to the individual squares of card but this time don't draw any pictures.

Play the game

Each player takes one of the large cards and the smaller cards are turned face downwards on to the table.

The first player picks up a small card and reads the word out loud. If he finds that this small word card matches a word on his big card then he puts it on top of the word. If it does not match, then the player replaces the card face downwards on the table and the next player takes a turn. The first player to cover up all the words on the big card is the winner.

The take-a-word game

Collect together:

- several small pieces of card, 10cm by 6cm. (To make the game worthwhile you will need at least 5 cards.)
- a black felt tip pen.

Make the game

1 On one side of each of the pieces of card write a content word that you are introducing at the moment. Remember to use lower-case letters.
2 On the other side of the cards write out some simple instructions or questions, e.g.
    Jump up and down 10 times.
    Who had to get home by 12 o'clock?
    Run to your bedroom and back.

Play the game

Place the cards word side up at one end of the room and stand with your child as far away from them as possible. Name one of the words and ask your child to run to the cards and bring it back for you. If he returns with the correct word he should then carry out the instruction or answer the question contained on the back of the card. If he does this correctly he scores a point and keeps the card. If the child returns with the wrong card ask him to take it back and try again. (A little help may be necessary to begin with.)

This is a super game for boisterous children.

Word skittles

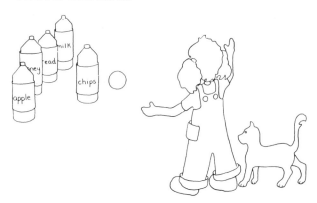

Collect together:

- large, empty washing-up liquid bottles. You will need at least five.
- Sellotape.
- a few sheets of paper, 30cm by 22cm. (You need as many sheets of paper as there are bottles.)
- scissors.
- a felt tip pen.
- a ball.

Make the game

1 Wrap a sheet of paper round the middle of each bottle and sellotape it into position.
2 Using large clear lower-case letters write a content word on to the front of each bottle.

Play the game

Stand the bottles up in a group and ask the child to see how many skittles he can knock down with the ball. He scores a point for every bottle he knocks down, providing he can say the word on the bottle.

Win the word

(To make a game for two players)

Collect together:

- 10 pieces of stiff white paper or card, 15cm by 5cm.
- a felt tip pen.
- 2 sentence racks. Detailed instructions for making the racks can be found in stage three.
- a ruler.

Make the game

1 Choose 10 content words. Write each word

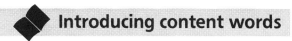

on one of the cards, placing the words exactly 7cm from the bottom of each card. Draw a simple picture above each word.

2 On the back of the cards, write out the words again. Place the words 7cm from the bottom of each card but this time, don't draw a picture.

Play the game

Two players sit opposite each other.

Each player takes 5 of the cards and puts them in the cardboard sentence rack so that he can see the words and pictures but his opponent can see only the words.

Both players place their hands behind their backs.

The first player asks, 'Where have I hidden the…cat?' Both players quickly point to the 'cat' card and the one who gets there first keeps the card.

Hands are again put behind backs and the winner then asks, 'Where have I hidden the…ball?'

The overall winner is the one with the most cards.

Word pairs

Collect together:

● 12 small pieces of card, 7cm by 7cm.
● a felt tip pen.

Make the game

1 Decide on 6 content words, e.g. mummy, daddy, dog, Nick, Kate, Sophie.
2 Write each word on to two of the pieces of card, so that you have two cards with mummy on, two with daddy on and so on.
3 If you feel it is necessary you could also draw

some pictures of mummy, daddy, etc. just above the printed words. However, if you do this, you will need larger pieces of card.

Play the game

Place the cards word side down on to the table or floor. The child picks up one card and says the word. He then picks up another card and says the word. If the two words are the same he can keep them. If not he puts them back face downwards on to the table.

Simple recipe cards

Collect together:

● a sheet of paper or card, 15cm by 35cm.
● felt tip pens.
● a ruler.
● the ingredients and utensils needed for your recipe.

Make the game

Using symbols, numbers and a limited number

of appropriate words, make a simple recipe card for your child to use.

As you can see from the illustrated 'Cheese scone recipe card' very few words are used and children soon become adept at interpreting the illustrations and symbols. However, do make sure the recipe you select is as simple as possible and always set out the instructions on the card from left to right.

Play the game

Provide the child with the recipe card, necessary equipment and ingredients. Be on hand to help interpret the card and to put the scones into and out of the oven.

Shopping lists

The next time you go shopping for a few groceries ask your child to help you make a shopping list. Use a large sheet of paper and down one half of the paper write out the names

of the items you need. Remember to use lower-case letters and make sure the words are large and clear. As you write out each word tell your child what it is and ask her to repeat the word. Ask your child to draw a little picture of each item next to the appropriate word, or alternatively you could draw the pictures and she could colour them in.

When you go shopping take a pencil with you. As each item is placed in the shopping basket, ask your child to place a tick against the correct word on the list. The pictures should help her to remember the words.

Word snakes and ladders

Collect together:

● a snakes and ladders board.
● a pack of 20, 6cm by 6cm blank cards.
● a felt tip pen.
● some counters or buttons.

Make the game

Write a content word on each of the 20 cards. You may use the same word several times if you like and you may need to add simple pictures to help your child recognise the words. Add a number (from 1 to 5) on the corner of each card.

Play the game

When playing snakes and ladders, use the pack of cards instead of a dice. Shuffle the cards and lay the pack face downwards on the table. Each player draws the top card from the pack and the number on the card indicates his next move. the child should attempt to read the word before moving his counter.

Word donkey

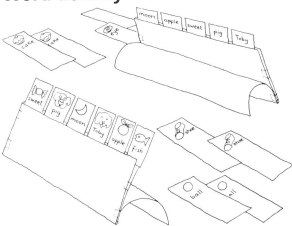

(To make a game for two players)

Collect together:

- 20 pieces of card, 14cm by 15cm.
- 2 sentence racks. Instructions for making the racks can be found in stage three.
- a felt tip pen.

Make the game

1 Decide on 10 contents words.
2 Write each content word on two cards. The words should be 7cm from the bottom of each card. Draw a simple picture above the words.
3 On the back of each card write out the words again but this time don't draw a picture.

Play the game

The two players sit opposite each other. Each player has a sentence rack. One of the cards is removed from the pack and the remaining cards are divided between the two players. The players then look through their cards and put on one side any matching pairs of cards they find.

The remaining cards are put in the sentence racks so that the player can see his pictures but his opponent sees only the word on the back. The players then take turns to point to a word they think they need saying, 'Please may I have the word...car.' If they identify the word correctly they may take the card and put on one side any pairs they make. The loser is the person left with the odd card.

A pretend shop

Decide on what sort of shop your child would like to have...a grocery shop, a shoe shop, a clothes shop or perhaps a toy shop?

When you have decided, collect together as many appropriate items as possible and arrange them on a table top. If you have a toy cash register put this in the shop, but if you haven't, an empty box will do just as well. Children love to handle real money, so if you can, give them a handful of loose change. Failing this try giving them buttons or clean milk bottle tops to use as pretend money.

On some large pieces of card, write out the names of some of the items in the shop. Use large, clear, lower-case letters and remember to put the price of the item underneath the word. On two more pieces of card, write out the words 'open' and 'closed'. Together with your child put the label on the items in the shop. You will also need a shopping bag and a purse.

Start to play the shopping game. Whenever possible point to and name the words on the table top but don't be too pedantic about this; you don't want to spoil imaginative play. Use the open and closed notices and take turns at being shop-keeper and customer.

Colour labels

Collect together:

- 16 pieces of 10cm by 5cm card.
- 8 different coloured pencil crayons, e.g. black, red, blue, green, yellow, pink, orange, brown.

Make the game

Take the blank cards and write various colour words on them using the appropriately coloured pencil crayons.

Play the game

Give the child the cards and ask him to look around the house and label colourful items with the correct colour word, e.g. he could put a 'blue' label on his bedspread and a 'green' label on a bowl full of apples.

At a later stage you could make a second set of cards using a black felt tip pen, which wouldn't provide a colour clue to the word.

Colour by words

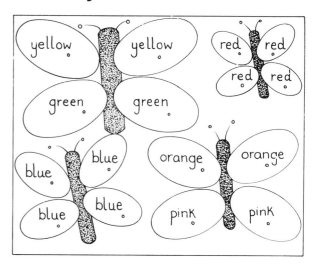

Collect together:

- a sheet of paper, 25cm by 20cm.
- a felt tip pen.
- crayons.

Make the game

1 Draw a very simple picture on to the sheet of paper, e.g. a butterfly.

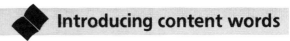

2 Write some colour words, e.g. red, blue, green, on the different sections of the butterfly's wings.

Play the game

Give the child the picture and some crayons. Ask her to colour in the butterfly's wings using the correct colours. If the words are new to the child, it might help if you put a small dot of the appropriate colour next to each colour word.

Colour lotto

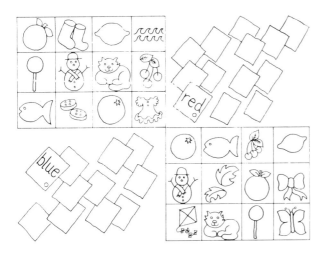

(To make a game for two players)

Collect together:

- 2 large pieces of card, 30cm by 20cm.
- 24 small pieces of card, 5cm by 10cm.
- a ruler.
- felt tip pen.
- crayons.

Make the game

1 With the pen and ruler, divide each of the

large cards into 12 equal sections. Each section should be 5cm by 10cm.
2 In each section draw an animal or object you would associate with a particular colour, e.g. a red apple, a white snowman, a black cat, etc. Colour the pictures in.
3 On the small pieces of card write the names of the colours you have used. Remember to use lower-case letters and, if it would help your child, you could put a small dot of the appropriate colour next to the word.

Play the game

Place the small cards word-side downwards on the table top. Each player takes it in turn to pick up a word card. If the player finds that the colour word corresponds to a colour picture on his large card he puts the word on top of the picture. If the word doesn't match any of his pictures, he replaces the word face downwards on the table. The first player to cover all his pictures is the winner.

* A sounds table

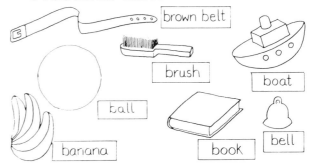

Together with your child, decide on a sound, e.g. 'b'. Look around your home and collect together any objects which start with the sound...b, e.g. ball, banana, bat, a brown belt. Arrange the objects on a table top and label them.

* A sounds bag

Collect together:

- an old pillowcase.
- a collection of objects, e.g. an apple, a fork, a pencil, a toy car, etc.

Play the game

Put one of the objects (e.g. an apple) into the pillowcase without the child seeing what it is. Ask the child to put her hand in the bag and feel for the object. Tell her that the object starts with the sound 'a', and ask her if she can tell you what the object is. If she guesses correctly, take the apple out and put something else in the bag.

Later, when the child is a little more sure of her initial letter sounds, you can ask her to tell you what sound the object in the bag starts with.

* I spy sounds

Play the game

If you have a couple of minutes to waste, e.g. while waiting in the doctor's waiting room or while peeling the potatoes, the traditional game of I spy is a valuable game to play with your child. Do remember to use the sound and not the name of the initial letter and it also helps little children if you also give a clue, e.g. 'I spy with my little eye something on my face beginning with...n...'

Number word sorting

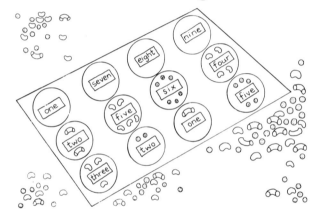

Collect together:

- a bun tin with a dozen sections.
- a handful of assorted dried peas, rice and beans. (Don't use dried red kidney beans as these are dangerous if swallowed.)
- 12 small pieces of paper, 3cm by 2cm.
- a felt tip pen.
- Sellotape.

Make the game

Write some number words, e.g. one, two, three, etc. on the small pieces of paper and sellotape the words inside the sections in the bun tin.

Play the game

Give the child the dried peas and beans. Ask him

to read the different numbers and to place the correct number of peas in each section. You will of course need to give your child quite a lot of help at first as he will not only be coping with new words but he will also be dealing with the concept of number.

Jump! Skip! Hop!

Collect together:

- 7 pieces of 20cm by 8cm card.
- a felt tip pen.

Make the game

Write some action words on the blank cards, e.g. jump, run, walk, hop, skip, crawl, roll.

Play the game

There are two versions of this game; you can play it either indoors or out.

The indoor version
Clear as large a space as possible in the centre of the room. The adult should hold up one card at a time and ask the child to read the card and carry out the action. If the child does this successfully, he keeps the card. The aim of the game is for the child to win all the cards. Obviously adults should also take a turn at carrying out the action words.

The outdoor version
You will need a large grassy area. Lay the cards at intervals either in a long line or, if space won't permit this, around the perimeter of your lawn. Your child picks up the first card, e.g. jump. He then jumps to the next card and continues to read and carry out the instructions until he has completed the course.

Stage three:
Introducing connecting words

Putting words together

By this stage your child should be able to 'look-and-say' quite a number of separate 'content' words, e.g. mummy, daddy. You can now begin to use 'connecting words' (e.g. 'and' 'the') to string the 'content' words together to form simple phrases, e.g. 'mummy and daddy'.

The decision as to which connecting words to introduce first has been simplified for us by the work of J. McNally and W. Murray, who have drawn up a 'key words' list. Although most adults know about 20,000 different words, McNally and Murray have shown that the following 12 words make up a quarter of what we read and write.

a, and, he, I, is, in, of, it, the, that, was, to.

McNally and Murray's key words list (part of which is reproduced in this section) shows that these 12 words plus a further 20 words make up a third of all we read. It would therefore be sensible when introducing 'connecting' words to choose words from the key words list. Indeed many published reading schemes for children do just that

How to introduce 'connecting' words. . .

To put the word 'and' on a look-and-say card and ask the child to learn it out of context is pointless since it will have no meaning. Therefore dispense with the look-and-say cards at this stage and concentrate on using your chosen 'connecting' words in the games and activities described in this section.

A key word list

The words are grouped in order of written frequency. The first 32 words make up a third of all you read.

a, and, he, I, in, is, it, of, that, the, to, was.

all, as, at, but, are, for, had, have, him, his, not, on, one, said, so, they, we, with, you.

about, an, back, been, before, big, by, call, came, can, come, could, did, do, down, first, from, get, go, has, her, here, if, into, just, like, little, book, made, make, me, more, much, must, my, no, new, now, off, only, or, our, other, out, over, right, see, she, some, their, them, then, there, this, two, when, up, want, well, went, were, what, where, which, who, will, your.

A treasure hunt

Collect together:

- several sheets of paper.
- a felt tip pen.
- treasure, e.g. an apple, a biscuit or a 5p coin.

Play the game

The aim of the game is to give the child written clues which she will follow in order to find the treasure. For example, on the first sheet of paper you could write 'look in the kitchen'. In the kitchen the child would find a second sheet of paper saying 'look on the television' and so on. Eventually after following all the instructions the child finds the treasure. This game is great fun for energetic children especially if some of the clues are out in the garden.

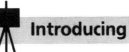

A child's own word file

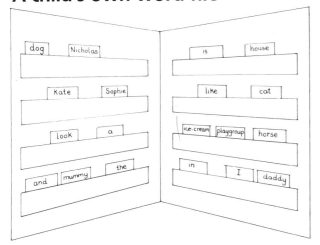

and new words can easily be added to the collection. The words from this file can also be used with the 'sentence rack' to make simple sentences.

A sentence rack

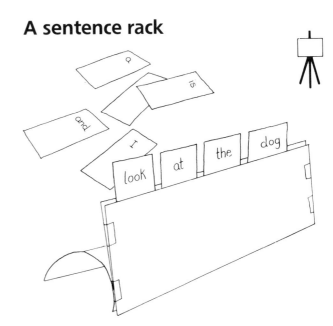

Collect together:

- a sheet of card, 44cm by 32cm.
- 8 strips of card, 20cm by 3cm
- Sellotape.
- small rectangles of card, 6cm by 3cm.
- a felt tip pen.

To make the file

Fold the large sheet of card in half to make a folder. Inside the folder turn the strips of card into long pockets by sellotaping each strip down on three sides. Make sure that the strips are not too close together. You should be able to get 4 strips on each half of the folder.

On the top half of each of the little rectangles of card print a word that your child can read or one that you are introducing at the moment.

Slip the little word cards into the pockets on the folder so that the words can be seen.

Using the word file

Your child now has instant access to his words

Collect together:

- a piece of card, 10cm by 25cm.
- Sellotape.
- a long cardboard tube. The tube needs to be 25cm long.
- scissors.

Make the rack by:

1 Cutting the cardboard tube in half along its length. Keep one half and discard the other.
2 Fold the piece of card in half along its length and stick the ends together with Sellotape so that you have a double thickness of card.
3 Lay the tube cut side down on a table top and sellotape the folded cardboard strip

uppermost. The tube prevents the card from falling over.

Using the sentence rack

The child can now stand the little word cards (taken from his own word file) in the sentence rack to form simple sentences. The rack is also used in various word games found in this book.

Word bricks

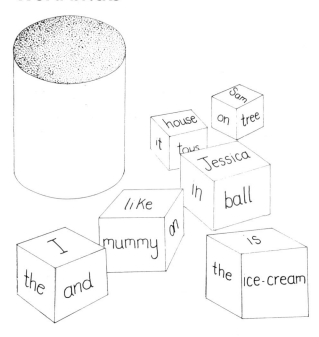

Collect together:

- 6 children's wooden bricks.
- a black felt tip pen.
- some counters or buttons.
- an empty tin.

Make the game

Write some of the words your child has learnt on

to the bricks. One word for each side of the cube. For every 'content' word e.g. 'dog', write two 'connecting words'. Obviously you can repeat common ones such as 'and', 'is', and 'the'.

Play the game

Put the bricks in a tin, give the tin a good shake and tip the bricks out. Can the child make a sentence from any of the top words on the bricks? If he can, he scores a point and takes a counter. If not, he puts the bricks back in the tin and the next player takes a turn.

Build a sentence game

Collect together:

- a few sheets of paper.
- a felt tip pen.
- several small pieces of card, 5cm by 5cm. The exact number of cards will rather depend upon the number of words used in the sentences.
- a pencil.

Make the game

1 Using a few words from the 'key words list' and the content words your child has learnt, write out two or three simple sentences on the individual sheets of paper, e.g.
    Kate and Sophie are in the garden.
    Nicky is in the house.
    Toby and Jessica are playing ball.
2 Write all the words from the sentences on to the individual pieces of card.

Play the game

Each player is given a sheet of sentences to look at. Read through the sentences together so that the child is familiar with all the words. Place the individual word cards face downwards in the centre of the table

The first player lifts a word card and if it corresponds to the first word in any of his sentences he keeps the card, places it on the table in front of him and, using the pencil, crosses the word off his sheet of sentences. The next player then takes a turn.

The aim of the game is for the child to build up a complete sentence from the individual cards, using the sentences on the paper as a reference.

If a player lifts a card and it is not the next word in any of his sentences he returns the card face downwards on the table top. The winner is the one who completes all his sentences first.

A letter in the post

Children love to receive a real letter in the post. The letter can be from Father Christmas (even during the summer months children like to hear from Santa), from a pet, from Gran, or simply

from you. When writing the letter remember to keep the sentences short and simple and use lots of familiar content words. Little illustrations can help the child to remember words, as well as making the letter more interesting to look at.

When the postman has been, read the letter together. As you read, run your finger underneath each word, this helps to train the childs eye to scan from left to right. If you wish, you could help your child to write a simple reply, but do remember to use lower-case letters.

Sentence and picture matching

Collect together:

- 5 pieces of 20cm by 5cm card.
- 5 pieces of 10cm by 10cm card.
- a felt tip pen.
- crayons.

Make the game

1 On each of the 20cm by 5cm pieces of card, write a simple sentence using the content

words your child already knows and a limited number of connecting words taken from the key word list, e.g.

> I like the dog.
> I like mummy and daddy.
> I like ice-cream.

2 On the square cards draw a simple picture to illustrate each sentence. Your child might like to colour the pictures in.

Play the game

Together with your child read the sentences and look at the pictures. When your child seems confident with the new words ask him to match each picture with the appropriate sentence.

The missing word game

Collect together:

- a few sheets of paper, 30cm by 25cm. You will need one sheet of paper for each player.
- a felt tip pen.
- several small pieces of card, 5cm by 3cm. The exact number of cards will rather depend on the number of missing words you use in the sentences.

Make the game

1 On each of the large sheets of paper write two or three simple sentences but miss out one word from each sentence. (The words in the sentences should be taken from the key word list, and also from the child's content word list.) The space where the missing word should be, needs to be 6cm long.
2 Write out the missing words on to the individual small cards.

Play the game

To begin with, help the child to place the missing words in the sentences and read sentences together.

Remove the small cards, shuffle them and put them in a pile in the centre of the table. Each player takes a turn at lifting a card and if the word is one of his missing ones he places it in his sentence. if it isn't a word he needs he puts it back at the bottom of the pile.

The winner is the one who completes all his sentences first.

Home made reading books

- Home made reading books are inexpensive to make.
- They appeal to the child because the content can reflect her interests.
- They introduce new words at the child's own individual pace.
- Because the child has been actively involved in the production of the book, her motivation to read the book is high.

To make the book, either buy a plain sketch book or staple together sheets of white paper. Involve the child by first of all ascertaining what sort of book she would like to read, e.g. a fairy story, a football story or perhaps a story about one of her favourite toys.

Whatever type of book you decide on it should have plenty of pictures in it. These can be drawn by the child herself, or she could cut out photographs and stick them into the book. Be sure to leave enough space for the text.

The text should again be a joint effort between yourself and the child, but do remember to keep the sentences as simple as possible. Ask the child what she would like to say about each picture and then write down a simplified version underneath the illustration. The adult should write in the text, using large, clear lower-case letters. Ask the child to watch you while you write and say each word out loud as you write it.

One cannot over-emphasise the importance and impact of such books. As the child has been actively involved in the production of the book and as the sentences will be in essence her words, she should have little difficulty in reading the book with you. This in turn will give her plenty of reading confidence, which will benefit her greatly when she approaches published reading matter.

A sentence race game

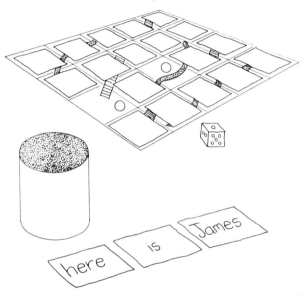

Collect together:

- the base board from a game such as snakes and ladders or ludo.
- small pieces of card. (You will need as many as there are squares on the board and they will also need to be the same size as the squares on the base board.)
- a dice.
- a felt tip pen.
- a counter for each player.

Make the game

1 On the small squares of card write out some of the content words your child already knows and some of the connecting words taken from the key words list. Obviously with so many cards to fill you will need to repeat some of the words.
2 Place the cards, word side up, on each of the squares on the base board.

Play the game

Each player takes turn at throwing the dice to determine how many spaces he moves. When a player lands on a square, he removes the word and keeps it safe. When he has sufficient words he tries to make a sentence with them. If he succeeds in making a sentence he may move his counter an extra space for each of the words in the sentence. After a sentence has been made the words are returned to the board on any vacant square.

The winner is the one to reach the end of the base board first.

Capital letter snap

(To make a game for two players)

Collect together:

- 24 pieces of 8cm by 8cm card.
- a felt tip pen.

Make the game

1 On twelve of the small cards write some of the words your child knows well, (one word per card). Don't use first names as these should have already been given an initial capital letter. Write the words out using lower-case letters.
2 Write the words out again on the remaining twelve cards but this time start each word with a capital letter.

Play the game

Shuffle the cards and divide them between the two players. The cards can be used to play the traditional game of snap but instead of calling out 'snap' the child calls out the word to win.

A diary chart

Collect together:

- a sheet of card 30cm by 30cm.
- 4 strips of 8cm by 2cm card.
- 14 strips of 7cm by 25cm card.
- a felt tip pen.
- Sellotape.

Make the game

1 At the top of the large sheet of card write the words 'Today is'. Just beneath the words sellotape two of the small 8cm by 2cm strips of card. The strips need to be placed in a vertical position, 20cm apart and the Sellotape should only be applied to the top and bottom of each strip.
2 Beneath the sellotaped strips, write the words 'I am' and below this sellotape the two remaining 8cm by 2cm cards, in a vertical position and 20cm apart.
3 On seven of the 7cm by 25cm cards write the names of the days of the week and use the remaining cards to describe various activities your child might regularly take part in, e.g. shopping, going to playgroup, going to the park, watching television etc.

Play the game

Hang the diary chart in a convenient place and occasionally help your child to fill in the chart by sliding the appropriate word cards underneath the sellotaped strips.

An interest scrap-book

If your child has a particular interest or hobby she may like to make an interest scrap-book. For example, if she has a pet and likes animals, her scrap book could contain photographs, drawings, postcards and leaflets which feature domestic pets.

Talk to your child about some of the photographs and ask her if she would like to include a few simple sentences in the scrap-book. (These should be written by the adult in large, clear, lower-case letters.) Let the child decide which pictures should have writing underneath and what should be written,

although you might find you will need to simplify the child's sentences a little.

* Sandpaper letters

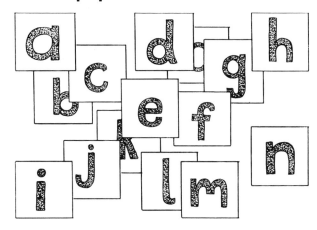

Collect together:

● 26 pieces of 10cm by 10cm card.
● several sheets of heavy grade sandpaper.
● a piece of chalk.
● scissors.
● glue and a glue brush.

Make the game

1 Using the chalk, draw the letters of the alphabet on the front of the sandpaper. Each letter needs to be 8cm high, lower-case, and double line thickness.
2 Cut round the outline of each letter and then stick them rough side up on to the cardboard squares. (One letter per square.)

Play the game

The sense of touch is most important to young children. The use of sandpaper letters develops this sense and uses it to familiarise the child with letters and the sounds they make.

Give the child one or two letters at a time, ask him to feel the letters with his finger tips and tell him what sounds the letters make. (Remember to use the sounds not the names of letters.)

When he has explored the letters sufficiently play the blindfold game. Cover the child's eyes, give him one of the letters and ask him to tell you by touch which letter he can feel. Take turns at playing the blindfold game and if you wish to make it a little bit more competitive you could award points for each correct guess.

* Sounds post box

Collect together:

- 5 empty shoe boxes with lids.
- a sharp knife or scissors for a grown-up.
- 30 pieces of 10cm by 10cm card.
- a felt tip pen.
- crayons or felt tip pens.
- Sellotape.
- 10 pieces of 5cm by 5cm paper.

Make the game

1 Using the scissors or sharp knife cut an 11cm by 2cm letter box opening at the end of the shoe boxes.
2 Print a lower-case letter on each of the pieces of paper and sellotape one of these into position below each letter box.
3 On the squares of card draw some simple colourful pictures of objects or animals whose names start with the letters printed on the shoe boxes, e.g. d = a picture of a dog. Alternatively you could cut out colourful pictures and stick these on to the cards.
4 Put the lids on the shoe boxes and stand them in a row on a convenient table top.

Play the game

Ask the child to post the picture post cards through the correct letter boxes. Lots of help will be needed at first, especially in discovering the initial letter sounds. You might like to print the initial letter on the back of each card.

An alternative use for the boxes would be to use the sandpaper letters described in this section and to post these through the correct boxes. Simple matching games of this type help familiarise the child with the letter shapes.

* Take-a-letter game

Collect together:

- 10 pieces of 6cm by 6cm card.
- a sheet of paper.
- a felt tip pen.

Make the game

1 Print a lower-case letter on each of the small pieces of card.
2 On the sheet of paper make a list of the

letters you have used and beside each one write an instruction or question, e.g.

a = Run upstairs and back.
b = Sing a nursery rhyme.
c = Who found a mouse under the Queen's chair?

Play the game

Place the cards letter side up at one end of the room and stand with your child and the list of instructions on the opposite side of the room. Ask your child to fetch one of the letters for you. Remember to use the sound and not the name of the letter. When the child returns with the correct letter, read out the appropriate instruction or question. If the child successfully carries out the instruction, she keeps the letter and scores a point.

A slight variation would be for the child to fetch any letter she chooses and then for her to tell you what sound the letter makes before you read out the task. If more than one child is involved they take turns at fetching the letters.

* Letter snap

Collect together:

- 52 pieces of 5cm by 5cm card.
- a felt tip pen.

Make the game

Write each letter of the alphabet on two of the pieces of card. Remember to use lower-case letters.

Play the game

Shuffle the cards and divide them between two players. The player should sit next to each other so that the letters can be seen the right way up.

The players take turns at placing a card on to the table top. Whenever a player sees a matching pair of letters he calls out the sound of the letter and wins the cards.

* Letter skittles

Collect together:

- 5 or 6 empty washing up liquid bottles.
- 5 or 6 sheets of white paper, 28cm by 22cm.
- Sellotape.
- a felt tip pen.
- a small ball.

Make the game

Using the Sellotape, stick the white paper round the outside of the bottles. Print a letter on the front of each bottle, making sure that you use lower-case letters not capitals. Stand the bottles up in a group and give the ball to the child.

Play the game

See how many bottles your child can knock down with the ball. He scores a point for every bottle he knocks over, providing he can give you a word starting with the letter on the fallen bottle, e.g. 'b'... banana. Keep a tally of his and your score on a piece of paper.

Stand all the bottles up and start again. If he knocks 'b' down a second time he must think of a second word beginning with 'b'.

* Spin-a-letter

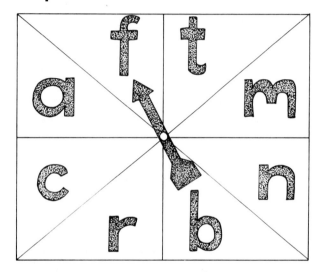

Collect together:

- a 22cm by 22cm piece of card.
- a 15cm by 2cm piece of card.
- felt tip pen.
- scissors.
- a brass fastener.
- a ruler.
- a box of buttons or milk bottle tops.

Make the game

1 Divide the large piece of card into eight sections by drawing a Union Jack. In each section print a lower-case letter.
2 Draw and cut out an arrow from the 15cm by

2cm piece of card. Attach the arrow to the centre of the Union Jack with the paper fastener. Do make sure the arrow will spin.

Play the game

Players take turns at spinning the arrow. When the arrow stops spinning, the player must say out loud the sound of the letter which the arrow points to and she must think of a word which starts with the same sound.

If you like you can have a word 'theme', e.g. all the words used by the players must be food names. Words must not be repeated and each player takes a button and earns a point for every correct word.

A time limit should be set and at the end of that time the buttons should be counted. The winner is the one with the most buttons.

* A sounds scrap book

Collect together:

- a scrap book.
- a felt tip pen.
- scissors.
- glue and glue brush.

Play the game

Devote a page of the scrap book to each sound. Start with 'a' and work through the alphabet. Using lower-case letters print a letter at the top of every page.

Over a period of time help your child to fill the scrap book with pictures of objects which start with the appropriate sound. The pictures can be cut from old magazines, catalogues, and leaflets. Try to avoid objects which don't actually start with the regular letter, e.g. for the f page cut out a fish and a fork but not a phone.

* Sounds lotto 2

(To make the game for two players)

Collect together:

- 2 pieces of 24cm by 12cm card.
- 16 pieces of 5cm by 5cm card.
- a ruler.
- a felt tip pen.
- crayons or felt tip pens.

Make the game

1 Divide each 24cm by 12cm sheet of card into eight equal sections. Each section should measure 6cm by 6cm.
2 Decide on 16 letters you wish to introduce, and write these out in the sections on the large cards. You may prefer to use fewer letters, in which case you simply use a letter twice. (Do remember to use lower-case letters.)
3 On the small pieces of card draw pictures of animals or objects whose names start with the initial letters printed on the large cards. If you aren't particularly artistic you could cut out pictures from comics or magazines and stick them on to the cards.

Play the game

Give each player a letters card and turn the picture cards face downwards on the table. Each player takes it in turn to pick up a picture card and if the initial letter sound of the object is the same as a letter on his card, he places the picture on top of the letter. If the picture doesn't match with any of the letters on his card the player returns the picture face downwards on the table and the next player takes his turn.

The winner is the first one to cover up all his letters with pictures.

Please note, lots of help is needed at first to 'hear' the initial sound in a name. A grown-up should slowly say the name of the object or animal to the child, with the emphasis on the initial letter sound.

How to choose and use a reading book

Listening to your child read is one of the most productive, educationally valuable activities you can provide. Children who read regularly to their parents improve their reading skills and soon move on to the second phase of being able to read alone.

Choose your child's first 'reading' books on your own. Children don't realise their own limitations when first starting to read. They may well pick up and fall in love with books which are totally unreadable in terms of reading age and then you have the tricky problem of gently persuading them that a particular book is unsuitable. Of course the child should have plenty of opportunity to choose books at the local library or when spending her birthday book token.

Many large bookshops and book departments in large stores have educational sections where simple, colourful reading material can be found. Buy several books at the same time. Once your child starts to read, she will want to progress from one book to the next quite quickly and as the length of the text in these books is deliberately limited, progress tends to be rapid. It is sometimes best to opt for one particular 'reading scheme' initially and to buy several graded books at the first level. The advantage of this is that such schemes introduce new words very gradually, have lots of material at the same level and repeat words frequently. It is important that the child has plenty of books to read but does not over-reach herself by being faced with too many new words at once.

What to look for in a first reading book:

1 The books should be interesting and relevant to your child. Certain schemes do feature one-parent families or ethnic children. Try to match the book with the child.
2 The book should look bright and exciting, with colourful illustrations.
3 There should be no more than ten words to a page and if it is a 'first reader' considerably less, i.e. three or four.
4 The text should repeat words frequently.
5 The text shoud be large, clear, well laid out, and use lower-case letters.

How to the use the books

Before presenting the reading book to your child, look through the books and see if there are any new words in the text which your child doesn't already know. Use these new words in some of the games and activities listed in this book. It is important in the initial stages of learning to read that your child is 'successful'. She must know the words in the books she is presented with. Failure or a struggle at this early

stage is not to be contemplated. The aim is to provide an emotionally positive experience.

When you are sure that the child knows all the words in the book, find a time during the day when you can sit quietly without distraction and look at the book together. Look at the pictures and read the book to the child. Move your finger from left to right under the words as you read. Finally, ask her to read some of the book to you and as she reads help her to move her finger underneath the words. Remember that reading sessions should be short and frequent.

If your child seems to be 'stuck' on a particular word, wait ten seconds. This allows the child some time to think about the word. If the child still seems unable to proceed, quietly say the word for her. It's vital that the child doesn't feel she has failed to read and this can be avoided if during these initial reading experiences you foster the idea that it is a shared activity. Any word which seems to be persistently causing problems can then be practised in a few reading games.

As reading progresses, the need for learning the words prior to reading the book is greatly reduced. As the child builds up her reading vocabulary and her understanding of phonics she will be able to happily 'discover' new words. A more detailed account of this process is given in stage four.

If subsequent reading books have several lines of writing to a page, a small piece of card can be used to separate the lines. The card is placed just under the line of writing your child is reading.

Your child's first reading book is a tremendously important event. It is her first step on the road to literacy. So let her know just how proud you are of her achievement. Hopefully this book will be the first of many she will enjoy.

Stage four:
The beginnings of phonics

Sounds in reading

Long before a child is ready to break a word
down into individual sounds, you can be helping
him to 'hear' the difference between sounds.
The phonic activities and games in stages one,
two and three were designed to encourage the
child to listen to and distinguish between
different sounds.

The 'look-and-say' method gives a child a
quick and easy start to the process of learning to
read. However, by the time he has memorised
and can read just over 100 words, he may well
enjoy being able to discover new words for
himself. He may do this by any of the following
means:

A picture or the context may help him to
guess the correct word. Guessing in this way
is to be encouraged.

He could see a similarity between a known word
and a new word, e.g. bike and like.

He may notice that some words are used as a
part of bigger words, e.g. 'in' ... 'into'. Or he
may know both 'in' and 'to' individually but
have never put them together before.

Or he may break a word down into individual
sounds.

Stage four introduces games and activities
designed to help your child to break words
down into their sounds and then to build words
for himself by using sounds.

A sounds check list

It is important to use the regular sounds of
letters rather than their names, e.g. 'a', 'buh',
'cuh', 'duh', etc. By doing this you will be
helping the child to hear the sounds within
words, which will help tremendously when the
time comes for him to discover new words by
breaking them down into separate units.

Make sure that you are sounding out the
letters correctly by reading aloud the following
list of words. The sound that the initial letter
makes is the sound to use for that particular
letter.

a	a ... pple	apple
b	b ... ed	bed
c	c ... at	cat
d	d ... og	dog
e	e ... gg	egg
f	f ... ish	fish
g	g ... ot	got
h	h ... at	hat
i	i ... ll	ill
j	j ... ug	jug
k	k ... ing	king
l	l ... id	lid
m	m ... an	man
n	n ... ot	not
o	o ... n	on
p	p ... an	pan
q	qu ... een	queen
r	r ... at	rat
s	s ... un	sun
sh	sh ... op	shop
t	t ... ip	tip
th	th ... ink	think
th	th ... is	this
u	u ... p	up

v	v … an	van
w	w … et	wet
x	x does not make its regular sound as an initial letter. You can hear the sound it makes at the ends of words, e.g. bo … x, mi … x	
y	y … es	yes
z	z … oo	zoo

These are the sounds which you should practise with your child in the games and activities described in stage four.

When your child is completely confident with these regular sounds, you can gradually introduce long vowels, diphthongs and blends but this will normally be at a much later stage. N.B. The lists below give examples of these sounds. There are often many different ways of spelling each sound, but remember that it is the sound not the spelling which is important at this stage. For example, the first 'long vowel' given below is 'ee' as in 'see', this sound can also be spelt 'ea' as in 'sea'. What is important is that the child learns to recognise 'see' (or 'sea') as the sound 's' and the sound 'ee'.

Long Vowels

ee … see
ar … art
or … order
oo … soon
ur … fur

Diphthongs (combinations of vowel sounds)

i … ice
a … ape
oy … toy
o … open
air … hair
ow … now
ear … hear

Blends (combinations of two consonant sounds)

bl … blink	br … brown	ch … church
cl … clear	cr … crown	dr … drink
fl … flower	fr … frog	gl … glue
gr … green	ing … king	pr … present
pl … play	sl … slip	tr … tree

Spot the odd sound game

Collect together:

- 20 pieces of 8cm by 8cm card.
- felt tip pens.

Make the game

1 Decide on four sounds, e.g. 'h', 'f', 't', 'b'. On the small cards, draw five pictures for each sound, e.g.

> 'h' … horse, house, hat, hen, hand.
> 'f' … fish, face, fox, finger, feather.
> 't' … table, teapot, teeth, tomato, tiger.
> 'b' … bus, bottle, bee, boot, box.

2 On the back of each picture card print the intial sound.

Play the game

Place five of the cards all starting with the same sound, picture side up, in a row. Add a sixth card from another sound group. Ask the child to spot the picture starting with a different sound.

You will of course have to help the child at first by slowly saying the names of the objects out loud. The child can check for himself whether or not he has picked the correct picture by turning the cards over and looking at the letters printed on the back.

Sound pictures and three games

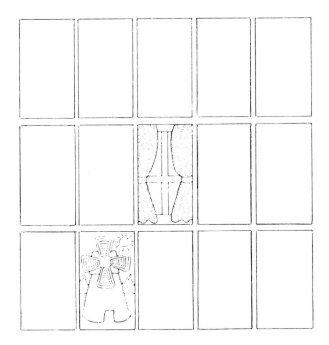

Collect together:

- 20 pieces of 8cm by 8cm card.
- felt tip pens.

Make the game

Think of ten sounds.

On the pieces of card draw some simple pictures of objects or animals which begin with sounds you have thought of. Use two cards for each initial letter, e.g.

'b' … Draw a picture of a bus and a bottle
'c' … A cup and a cat
's' … A sausage and a sun
't' … A teapot and a tent
'w' … A windmill and a window
'd' … A dog and a duck
'f' … A fish and a flower
'g' … A gate and a goat
'h' … A house and a hand
'l' … A ladder and a lorry

At a later stage you may like to make a second set of cards using some blends, e.g., ch … church and chip.

Play the games

Game one
Place the cards face downwards on a table top. The first player lifts and looks at two of the pictures and if they both start with the same sound he keeps the cards. If the initial sounds don't match, he returns the cards face downwards to the table.

The next player takes a turn.

The winner is the one who obtains the most cards.

Game two
Use the cards for a simple game of sound snap. Instead of calling out 'snap' the players should call out the sound.

Game three
Give the child the cards and ask her to sort them into pairs. Each pair starting with the same sound.

Building word cards

(To make a game for 2 players)

Collect together:

- 2 pieces of 18cm by 12cm card.
- 12 pieces of 5 cm by 5cm card.
- felt tip pens.
- a ruler.

Make the game

1 Divide each of the 2 large cards into 6 equal sections by drawing two lines down and two across. Each section should be 6cm by 4cm.
2 Think of six three-letter words, e.g. dog, cat, man, hen, gun, pig. In the first sections down the left hand side of the large cards, draw a small picture of each of the three-letter objects and at the side of the picture print the initial letter of the word.
3 On the 5cm by 5cm cards print out the remaining letters from each word.

Play the game

Give each player a large card. Turn the small cards face downwards on the table. The object of the game is to build up a complete word by placing the letters in the correct order in the sections on the large card, e.g. as the first letter of dog is already on the large card, the player must find the next letter, i.e. 'o'. He cannot put the 'g' down before the 'o' is in place.

Each player takes a turn at lifting one of the small letter cards. If the letter is the one he requires he places it in the correct section. If he doesn't need that particular letter, he returns it face downwards on the table. The winner is the one to build up all three words first.

Beat the clock

Collect together:

- several small pieces of card, 5cm by 5cm.
- a kitchen timer, or a watch with a second hand.
- a felt tip pen.
- 2 kitchen trays.

Make the game

1 Pick 3 or 4 words that your child knows well. Take the individual letters from these words and write them down on to the individual pieces of card.
2 Jumble the letters up on one of the two trays and put the tray at one end of the room. Put the empty tray on the opposite side of the room.

Play the game

Ask the child to stand by the tray of letters. Start the timer. (Use your own judgement on how long to allow for the building of each word.)

A grown-up should shout out one of the words to be made, e.g. 'dog'. The child has to then take the first letter of 'dog', i.e. 'd', run across the room and put it on the empty tray. He then returns for the next letter and so on until the word is complete. He should try to make the word before the timer buzzes!

Hide and seek words

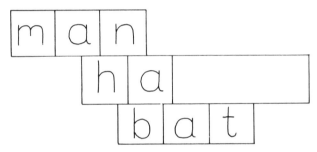

Collect together:

● 7 strips of 8cm by 20cm card.
● a felt tip pen.
● a ruler.

Make the game

1 Use the ruler and pen to divide six of the strips of card into three equal sections. Do this on the front and back of each card.
2 Think of twelve, three letter words and then write them down on six of the strips of card. (Write one word on each side of a strip with one letter in each section.)

Play the game

Take the blank strip of card and place it over one of the word strips. Slowly slide the blank across the word until you have exposed the first letter. Ask the child to tell you what sound he can see.

Continue to slide the card across the strip until the next letter in the word can be seen. Ask the child to say the two sounds together,

starting with the first sound. Finally expose the last letter and ask the child to say all the letters out loud again, and to say the complete word. This activity helps the child to recognise that words are built up from individual sounds.

Make a word game

Collect together:

● 6 toy bricks.
● a black, felt tip pen.
● some counters or buttons.
● an empty tin.

Make the game

Print some lower-case letters on to the bricks (one sound for each side of the cube) . You may like to repeat the vowels several times.

Play the game

Put the bricks into the tin, give the tin a good shake and tip the bricks out. Can your child make a word using any of the top letters on the bricks? Not all the letters have to be used each time. If he can make a word, he scores a point and takes a counter. If not, he puts the bricks back and the next player takes a turn. The winner is the one with the most counters after a given length of time.

The name game

This is a good game for car journeys. Decide on an initial sound, e.g. 'd', and a common group of objects, e.g. animals.

The first person thinks of an animal starting with 'd' e.g. dog. The next player thinks of a second animal, e.g. duck. The list of animals continues to grow longer until no more 'd' animals can be thought of.

Writing

Contents

Introduction

Before a child picks up a pencil and forms her first letters on paper, she should have aquired a good degree of manual pencil control and hand/eye co-ordination. We can help her to achieve such control with the introduction of some simple pre-writing games and activities.

A number of such games and activities are described in stage one of this writing section. Stage one provides lots of opportunities for pencil practice, but does not involve the use of letters. It complements the pre-reading section of this book and should be used in conjunction with the stage one pre-reading activities. (For advice on how your child should hold a pencil see stage two). At the same time, make sure that your child has plenty of access to jigsaws, paint and paper, chalk and crayons, posting boxes, building bricks and other manipulative, 'Lego' type games. You may also like to obtain 'chunky' crayons and pencils as these are obviously much easier for small hands to hold. Playing with Playdough and Plasticine also helps to develop hand muscles and co-ordination.

Stage two writing activities are concerned with the correct formation of letters and the writing of words. Writing goes hand in hand with reading and so the activities at this level should be used alongside those in stages two and three of the reading section.

It is also worth remembering that although reading and writing can be taught side by side, writing is in many ways a much harder skill for the child to master. Therefore her writing ability will almost certainly not be as advanced as her reading ability.

From the beginning, the correct formation of letters is vital, if the child is not to develop bad writing habits. Incorrectly formed letters will hamper her progress when she is old enough to use joined-up writing. It is just as easy for a child to learn to form a letter correctly as incorrectly; it is simply a matter of making sure that you help your child form the very first word. If you are not sure of the correct way to form some letters, study the 'letter chart' in stage two.

Stage one:
Pre-writing activities

A wet sand tray

We have all drawn pictures in the sand at the seaside. This activity enables the child to have the same fun at home.

Fill a large shallow tray or container with damp sand and encourage the child to draw pictures in the sand with her fingers. Silver sand is preferable, as builders sand tends to stain clothes. When one picture has been completed pat the sand smooth and start again.

Shaving foam pictures

Collect together:

- 1 spray can of shaving foam. (If you haven't got any shaving foam, you can make your own by whisking together soap flakes and a little warm water.)
- 1 smooth table top or tray.

Play the game

Put a generous squirt of foam on to the table top. Now for the fun! Encourage the child to spread the foam all over the table with his hands. Make pictures in the foam by using a finger to draw with. This looks especially good on dark surfaces.

When finished with one picture or pattern the child can spread the foam and start again. It's amazing where it gets spread to - but it's very easy to clear up.

Threading

Threading is a good pre-writing activity as it encourages hand and eye co-ordination and concentration.

To begin with, your child can thread a few empty cotton reels or cardboard rings (cut from a cardboard tube) on to a long bootlace. One end of the bootlace will need to be strengthened and the best way of doing this is to sellotape a used matchstick on to the end.

At a later stage the child can use a blunt ended darning needle to thread together large buttons and clean milk bottle tops.

A salt tray

Cover a tray or shallow container with a layer of salt. Encourage your child to draw pictures in the salt with her finger. The pictures will be more noticeable if the tray is dark in colour. To remove the picture gently shake the tray and start again.

A note of caution, do make sure your child has no small cuts on her hands before she starts.

Making a blackboard

Instead of buying a blackboard which can be very expensive and rather small, why not make one? The easiest method is to buy a large tin of 'blackboard paint' (available from good D.I.Y. shops) and simply paint part of an unpapered wall in your child's bedroom. The advantage of painting walls is that the blackboard area can be really large and at the right height for the child. What's more, it doesn't keep falling over! If you dislike the idea of a wall blackboard, paint as large a sheet of hardboard as you can find and stand this in your child's room. Provide lots of different coloured chalks and a duster.

Chalk is easy for small hands to hold, so children find it simple to use a blackboard. It can also provide a great a great deal of pleasure and enjoyment. A blackboard gives instant access to creative play and develops the imagination as it is often used in 'school' games. At a later stage it can also be used for 'real' writing practice.

Easy sewing cards

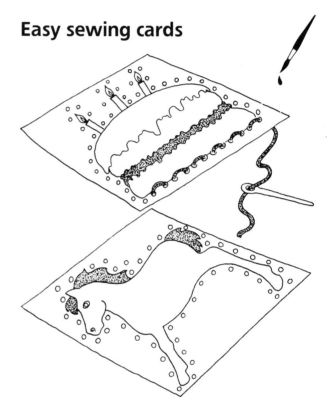

Collect together:

- 2 or 3 pieces of 15cm by 15cm thick card.
- a knitting needle or a pair of scissors.
- wool.
- a large blunt-ended darning needle.
- a felt tip pen.

Make the game

1 On the squares of card draw some simple, outline pictures of animals or objects.
2 Use the knitting needle or scissors to punch

holes round the outside of the pictures. The holes need to be about 2cm apart. (Obviously an adult had better do this.)

Play the game

Give the child the blunt needle threaded with wool and ask him to sew around the picture by pushing the needle through the holes.

Dot to dot

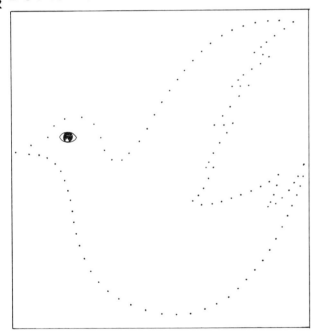

Collect together:

- pencils and paper.
- a black felt tip pen.
- a rubber.

Make the game

1 Using a pencil, draw the simple outline of an animal or object on to a sheet of paper.

2 Using the felt tip pen, draw dots round the outline about 1cm apart. Rub the pencil line out and you should be left with a dotted outline.

Play the game

Ask the child to join the dots together with his pencil.

Who caught the fish?

Collect together:

- a sheet of paper.
- a felt tip pen.
- a pencil.

Make the game

1 At the top of the sheet of paper draw a line of five or six pin-men figures and give each one a fishing rod. At the bottom of the paper draw a fish.
2 Draw curling, twisting, overlapping lines from the fishing rods down towards the fish but make sure that only one of the lines actually touches the fish.

Play the game

Ask the child to find out which of the figures has caught the fish by following the lines with her finger or pencil.

Copy patterns

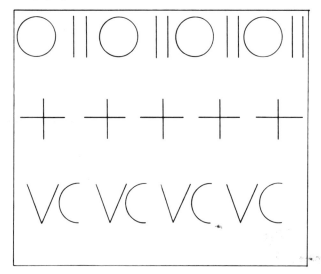

Collect together:

- a sheet of paper.
- a pencil.

Make the game

On the sheet of paper draw two or three lines of simple repeated pattern. It is best to start with a combination of straight lines and circles. Make sure that there is at least a 5cm gap between each line of pattern.

Play the game

Ask the child to copy your pattern by drawing in the gap between the lines. Make sure that he copies from left to right.

Tracing

Collect together:

- pencils and sheets of paper.
- greaseproof paper, cut to the same size as the sheets of paper.
- paper clips.
- a black felt tip pen.
- crayons.

Make the game

1 Use the felt tip pen to draw some simple pictures on the sheets of paper.
2 Cover each picture with a sheet of greaseproof paper and paper clip the greaseproof into position. Be sure that the paper clips don't obscure the picture.

Play the game

Ask the child to trace over the top of the picture with his pencil. He should try his best to keep the pencil on top of the felt tip pen lines. When the tracing is complete, the child can colour in his picture with the crayons.

Templates

Collect together:

- a large sheet of very thick card.
- a craft knife.
- pencils and paper.

Make the game

1 Draw the simple outlines of objects or animals on to the sheet of card. You could work to a theme, e.g. farm animals or transport. If you are not particularly artistic you could copy or trace pictures from books.
2 Using the craft knife, cut the shapes out. Obviously adults should make sure that small children don't handle such knives.

Play the game

The child can now draw round the templates on to a piece of paper. Afterwards the pictures can be coloured in.

Follow the road

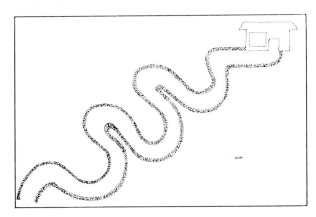

Collect together:

- pencils and paper.

Make the game

Draw a long twisting road on to the sheet of paper. To make it more interesting, draw something the child likes at the end of the road, e.g. a sweetshop. Do make sure that the road isn't too narrow - 2cm wide is ideal.

Play the game

Ask the child to take the pencil and draw a line from the start of the road to the sweetshop. Ask him to keep the pencil on the road at all times.

× Complete the face

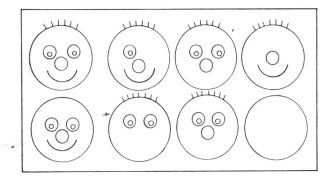

Collect together:

- pencils and paper.

Make the game

Draw some large circles on to a sheet of paper. Draw a simple complete face on the first circle; this gives the child a model to look at. Leave some circles blank and give the rest an incomplete face.

Play the game

Ask the child to complete the faces with her pencil.

Mazes

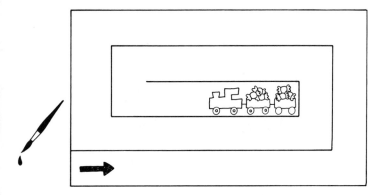

Collect together:

● pencils and paper.

Make the game

Draw a simple square maze on the sheet of paper. Put an arrow at the start of the maze and draw a favourite object in the centre.

Play the game

Ask the child to draw a line from the arrow to the centre of the maze without touching or crossing the lines. You could also offer a small reward, such as a Smartie or raisin, for a successful attempt.

Draw the other half

Collect together:

● pencils and paper.

Make the game

Draw the simple outline shape of everyday objects but leave one half missing. For very young children draw the complete shape but make one half dotted.

Play the game

Ask the child to complete the picture or join the dots.

Stage two:
riting activities

A letter chart

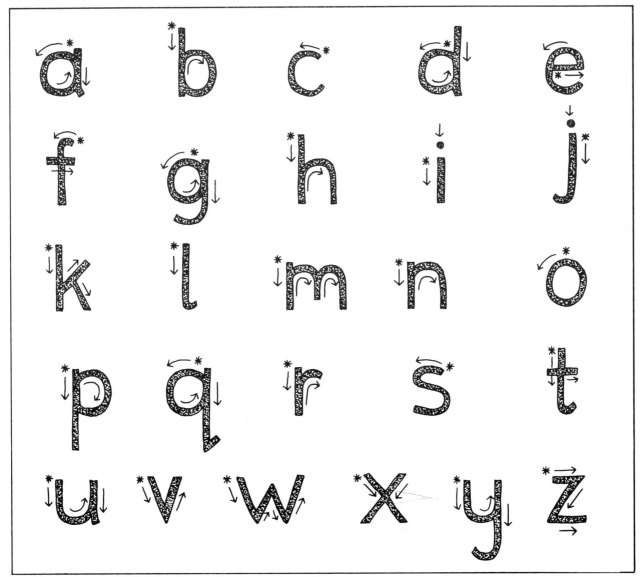

Start at the star and follow the arrows

Start with your child's name

The first word most children learn to read and to write is their own name. If your child has an especially long name it is often far better to allow them to start with a shortened version, e.g. Alex instead of Alexandra.

Write your child's name in large, clear letters on a sheet of paper. The first letter should be a capital but the rest should be lower-case. Starting with the first letter of your child's name, help your child to trace over the top of the letters with her index finger. Gently guide her finger and make sure that the finger forms the letters correctly. (See the letter chart if you are unsure of the correct formation of any letters.)

As you move her finger over the letters, talk about how she is forming each one, e.g. 'Let's start at the top of the 'S' and slide all the way down.' Do this a few times and then give her a pencil. Always use the sound and not the name of the letter. For a list of letter sounds see the sounds check list in stage four of the reading section.

Holding the pencil correctly is obviously important. She will find it much easier if she is sitting upright at a table in a comfortable position rather than sitting on the floor. The pencil should rest in between the first finger and the thumb, supported by the middle finger. Help her to go over the top of each letter with the pencil. Encourage her to form the letters

correctly and remember to talk about how she is forming them. Repeat this procedure a couple of times a day for several days, but only when the child seems enthusiastic and interested. Keep each writing session brief.

After writing directly over the top you can move on to writing over a dotted version of the name. Here the child joins dots together to form letters. Or you could place tracing paper on top of the name and ask your child to trace over it. As your child forms the letters, encourage her to say out loud the verbal instructions you rehearsed at the finger stage. Memorising the instructions in this way will ensure she forms the letters correctly when you are not guiding her.

By this time your child should be thoroughly familiar with each of the letters. You could now ask her to copy her name by writing underneath your own writing. It helps tremendously if you stay by her side during the first attempts at forming independent letters. Talk her through each letter just as you did when she was tracing with her finger.

When your child seems to be confidently copying underneath your letters, give her a card with her name on and ask her to copy from the card. With sufficient practice, most children will soon memorise the order and formation of the letters in their name and will be able to dispense with the card and write independently.

This procedure of finger tracing and copying can now be applied to other familiar words. The aim is slowly to introduce to your child all the letters of the alphabet.

Fingers first

When you have a few minutes to spare, play the fingers first game. Simply ask your child to write a word he knows well in the air with his finger. Ask him to imagine his index finger is a pencil

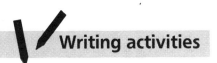

and remind him to form the letters correctly. Help him with any letters he seems unsure of, by holding his hand and gently guiding his finger.

To make the game more interesting, sit side by side with your child and ask him to write out a word or individual letter in the air while you try to guess what it is. Take turns at writing and guessing.

Word tracing cards

Collect together:

- a felt tip pen.
- a pencil.
- several sheets of card. (20cm by 15cm seems to be a good size for this activity.)
- several sheets of tracing paper or greaseproof paper. (They need to be the same size as the card you are using.)
- paper clips.

Make the game.

Using the words that your child is learning or has already learnt to read, make up a supply of word tracing cards which can be used for tracing whenever you child has a spare five minutes.

To make the cards more interesting you could draw appropriate pictures above the words and supply the child with crayons as well as a pencil.

1 Using large, clear, lower-case letters, print out a word on each of the pieces of card and draw an appropriate picture above the word.

2 Cover the cards with the tracing paper and paper clip the paper into position. Be sure that the paper clips don't obscure the word or picture. It will help your child to remember how to form the letters correctly if you put a little dot next to the starting point of each letter.

Dot to dot words

Collect together:

- sheets of paper.
- a felt tip pen.
- a pencil.
- a rubber.
- a crayon.

Make the game

1 Using the pencil, write some of the words that your child is currently learning on to the sheets of paper. Make sure that the letters are large, clear and lower-case. You could also include an appropriate picture above each word.
2 Use the felt tip pen to go over the outline of each letter and picture with small dots and then use the rubber to remove the pencil line.
3 Add a dot of colour to the starting point of each letter. This will help the child to remember how to form the letters correctly.

Play the game

Have a supply of dot to dot words and pictures available at all times so that the child can help herself to one if she feels inclined.

Cress letters

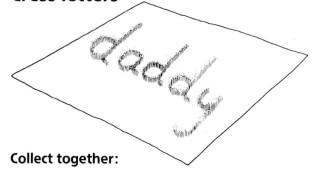

Collect together:

● a large plate.
● a pencil.
● blotting paper.
● mustard and cress seed.
● water.

Make the game

1 Help your child to write his name or any word which he is currently learning on to the sheet of blotting paper. The letters will need to be as large as possible.
2 Lay the blotting paper on to the plate and thoroughly dampen it with water.
3 Carefully spread the seeds on to the outline of the letters. Keep the blotting paper damp and watch the cress grow into the chosen word.

Opportunities for writing

It is important that your child should see writing as a valuable means of communication and expression. This will be helped if she is involved in as many writing activities as possible, for example, help her to:

● Write to gran and grandad. This is especially relevent if they live some distance away but even if they live just around the corner, writing a 'real' letter and posting it can be great fun;
● Write to a pen-friend;
● Send an invitation to a friend to come round to play or have tea;
● Make out simple shopping lists;
● Write a message in a birthday or Christmas card.
● Write to Father Christmas. This is always a very popular activity!
● Send a thank-you letter;
● Keep a diary;
● Write out some postcards while on holiday;
● Label her pictures with not only her name but a title as well;
● Write simple illustrated stories and poems.

No doubt you will find other types of writing that your child can do arising out of everyday activities. Encourage her as much as you can to see writing as something enjoyable and creative.